The World Council of Churches

Frits Albers

(March 1991)

Edited by Frank Calneggia

En Route Books and Media, LLC
Saint Louis, MO

⊕ENROUTE
Make the time

En Route Books and Media, LLC
5705 Rhodes Avenue
St. Louis, MO 63109

Contact us at
contactus@enroutebooksandmedia.com

Cover Credit: Ary Scheffer
"The Temptation of Christ" (1854)

Copyright 2026 Michael P. Albers

ISBN-13: 979-8-88870-502-5
Library of Congress Control Number: 2026933491

All rights reserved. No part of this book may be reproduced, stored in a retrieval system, or transmitted in any form, or by any means, electronic, mechanical, photocopying, or otherwise, without the prior written permission of the author.

Table of Contents

Introduction 1

Chapter One: The Fundamental Practice of the World Council of Churches 15

Chapter Two: The Fundamental Doctrine of the World Council of Churches 27

Chapter Three: The World Council of Churches and the "Everlasting Enmity" 43

Chapter Four: "... And with the Increase in Lawlessness, The Love of Many Shall Grow Cold" (Mt. 24:12) 63

Chapter Five: The Church of the New Age 89

Epilogue 101

Introduction

"He summoned his twelve disciples and gave them authority over unclean spirits with power to cast them out, and to cure all kinds of diseases and sickness. These are the names of the twelve apostles: first, Simon, who is called Peter, and his brother Andrew; James the son of Zebedee, and his brother John; Philip and Bartholomew; Thomas and Matthew the tax collector; James the son of Alphaeus, and Thaddaeus; Simon the Zealot, and Judas Iscariot, the one who was to betray him." (Mt. 10:1-4)

"And he sent them out to proclaim the Kingdom of God and to heal." (Lk. 9:2)

"So they set off to preach repentance; and they cast out many devils, and anointed many sick people with oil and cured them." (Mk. 6:12-13)

> "He said to (the eleven), 'All authority in heaven and on earth has been given to me. Go therefore instruct all the nations; baptise them in the name of the Father and of the Son and of the Holy Spirit, and teach them to observe all the commands I gave you'."
> (Mt. 28:18-20)

There has never been any doubt in the mind of the Holy, Catholic Church that with these words She stands before the whole of human history in the glory of Her Apostolic foundation, giving strength to the hierarchical structure of Her authority and mandate. And that here we are also at the beginning of Her unique Tradition. In 1991 there is still no rival on the horizon; neither of this Faith, nor of the message of this unique Catholic Church. And a thousand years hence it will still be the same.

> "After this the Lord appointed seventy-two others and sent them out ahead of Him, in pairs, to all the towns and places He Himself was to visit. He said to them, 'The harvest is rich, but the laborers are few; so ask the Lord

of the harvest to send laborers to his harvest. Go now but remember I am sending you out like lambs among wolves'. ... 'Anyone who listens to you listens to Me; anyone who rejects you rejects Me, and those who reject Me reject the One who sent Me'." (Lk. 10:1-3, 16)

Again there can be no doubt that 'The 72' stuck scrupulously to the message they had received from the Master, even to the way He had explained it to the Twelve. Yet on the other hand, it is equally certain that no objections were raised against the infallible way in which each of the Apostles had passed the message on to other followers in his own God-given way. There never were 72 x 12 different messages, nor 72 x 12 varieties of one fundamental misconception as we have now!

All during the centuries the Lord of the Harvest has dutifully sent many such 'groups of seventy-two' around the nations capable of grasping the immutable Message and to uphold within the context of the cultures of their times 'the Faith that comes to us from the Apostles'.

And so it came about that the sacred and unbreakable link with 'Peter', or whatever the name of the head of the Apostolic College at the time, remained scrupulously preserved by the members of only One Church with its one, unique Faith: "the beginning, foundation and root of ALL justification". [TRENT, VATICAN I]

And the result of the tireless efforts of the true successors of 'the 12 and their support groups of 72'?

> "After that I saw a huge number impossible to count of people from every nation, race, tribe and language. They were standing in front of the throne and of the Lamb, dressed in white robes .... These are the people who have been through The Great Persecution, and because they have washed their robes white again in the Blood of the Lamb, they now stand in front of God's throne and serve Him day and night in His Sanctuary. And the One who sits on the throne will spread His tent over them." (Rev. 7:9, 14-15)

Here we have that 'harvest', the divinely inspired reward for treasuring the only Faith that believes in an immutable Message which was formulated once and for all 2000 years ago and has been passed on in the infallible Tradition of only ONE Church.

And what about the alternative? Surely it cannot come as a major surprise that this Unique Faith, this Immutable Message and the Infallible Church founded by the Master are still as much intact today exactly as He gave them to us, due to the strength of His everlasting promise? This can certainly not be more amazing than that over all those centuries many of His followers must have closed their eyes to the bright Light of this Faith, changed the Immutable Message and abandoned the Church that guarded it, if we must now account for the existence of the World Council of Churches?

Since this priceless Faith, this unpolluted Message and this lone everlasting Structure are still with us today, does it not stand to reason that the divine reward for adhering to this triple uniqueness must be just as great as must be God's punishment on the colossal pretence of so many Catholics today, that this legitimate claim to distinctiveness can be safely ignored, and that in the search for religious unity no christian church may believe itself unique or claim to be in possession of that sought-after unity?

That talking about God's punishments for the organised effort to present this man-made arrogance as 'the new catholicism' in open defiance to a Divine Institution, may not be considered too strong, can be gathered from the following quotes.

> "And I saw another Beast coming up out of the earth. It had two horns like the Lamb, but it spoke like the Dragon. This second Beast was servant to the first Beast and extended its authority everywhere, making the world and all its people worship the first Beast ... Through the miracles which it was allowed to do on behalf of the first Beast, it was able to win over the people of the world and persuade them to erect a statue in honour of the Beast".
>
> "All those who worship the Beast and its statue ... will be made to drink the wine of God's fury, which is ready and undiluted ..." (Rev. 13:11-14, 14:9-10)

"I saw a strange church being built against every rule. No Angels were supervising the building operations. In that church nothing came from high above. Everything was done mechanically. Everything was being done according to human reason. I saw all sorts of people, things, doctrines and opinions in it. There was something proud, presumptuous AND COERCIVE about it all and they seemed to be very successful."

"I did not see a single Angel nor a single Saint helping in the work. Then I saw that everything that pertained to Protestantism was to be spread everywhere and was gradually gaining the upper hand. The Catholic religion fell into complete decadence. In those days Faith will fall very low and it will be preserved in some places only, in a few cottages and in a few families which God has protected from disasters and wars."

"I saw that many pastors allowed themselves to be taken up with ideas that were dangerous to the Church. They (those pastors) were building a great, strange, extravagant church. Everyone was to be admitted in order to be united and to have equal rights: evangelicals, Catholics, sects of every description. Such was to be the new church, but God had other designs". [1]

And in another page of that book Anna Catharina Emmerich is quoted as saying.

"I saw an enormous number of instruments brought into the church, and many persons, including children, had different tools as if trying to make something, but all was obscure, absurd and DEAD! Division and destruction reigned everywhere. I saw that many of the instruments in the new church, such as spears and darts, were meant to be used against the living Church. Everyone dragged in something different ..." (Op. cit)

---

[1] From *Life of Anna Catharina Emmerich*, by Rev. K. E. Schmoeger CSsR, with Ecclesiastical Approbation, 1867, 1868. On the command of Pope Pius IX, this book was translated into Italian.

"This organisation which formerly afforded such promising expectations, has been harnessed in its course by the modern enemies of the Church, and is now no more than a miserable effluent of the great movement of apostasy, being organised in every country for the establishment of a One-World Church, which shall have neither dogmas nor hierarchy neither discipline of the mind nor curb for the passions, and which, under the pretext of freedom and human dignity, would bring back to the world the reign of legalised cunning and brute force and of the oppression of the weak and of all those who toil and suffer".

"We know only too well the dark workshops in which are elaborated these mischievous doctrines which ought not seduce clear thinking minds."[2]

It is the clear observation of all Apostolic, Papal and Marian Catholics that the above quotes give the

---

[2] Pope St. Pius X. *Our Apostolic Mandate.* 1910.

most accurate description of the WORLD COUNCIL OF CHURCHES, aided and abetted in its work of global destruction of True Religion by active Catholic Modernists coming from the ranks of Cardinals, Archbishops, Bishops, Priests, Nuns and Brothers, hundreds of 'philosophers' and 'theologians', and a large percentage of the Catholic laity who have purposefully embraced a contraceptive 'lifestyle'.

In the West the destruction of Catholic education is all but complete, and the priestly formation at its secular institutes is so drenched with teilhardism that it is inevitable that most of its dribbling output will speak with a split tongue to promote ever so guardedly but very persuasively what St. John called 'the message of the Dragon': 'the gospel of the One-World Church'.

And just as we are able to gather from Sacred Scripture the rewards for faithfulness, so too we are able to obtain from the same sacred pages the punishments for unrepentance.

> "But the rest of the human race who escaped these plagues refused either to abandon the

things they had made with their own hands ... or to stop worshipping devils. Nor did they give up their murdering, or witchcraft, or fornication or stealing." (Rev. 9:20-21)

"... but though people were scorched by the fierce heat of it, they cursed the Name of God who had the power to cause such plagues, and they would not repent and praise Him." (Rev. 16:9)

"Men were biting their tongues for pain, but instead of repenting for what they had done, they cursed the God of Heaven." (Rev. 16:11)

"They cursed God for sending a plague of hail; it was the most terrible plague." (Rev. 16:21)

Mankind will never do or abandon for the sake of its own creation, as for example 'the New Catholicism' or the World Council of Churches, what it refuses to do, or to give up, in obedience to a Divine Institution, the Holy Catholic Church. Especially when such man-made structures are conceived by brains and used by forces in mortal combat with the Catholic Church. That is, for the preservation of 'the ultimate defiance' begun by the fallen angels before the foundation of the world, continued on earth in the 'everlasting enmity' established by God in Paradise between "The Woman of Genesis" and the "seed of Satan", and completed with the 'final unrepentance' endured for all eternity in Hell by both 'Satan and his seed'...

If this little book is about the World Council of Churches, it is even more so about the insanity of by far the great majority of Catholic men and women who by now have convinced themselves that a contraceptive lifestyle can be pleasing to God, and must be seen as the root of 'the new catholicism'. And it is above all about the ultimate in modern insanity: the strong conviction of all these modernist bishops and priests, men and women, that, when they are finally pushed out of the Catholic Church by the irresistible force of the Holy Spirit into the bowels of the World Council of Churches, that then they take the Catholic Church with them as 'the Catholic contribution' to the one-world religion of the of the one-world church, "doing everything in its power to subjugate the whole world to the tyranny of the first beast ..." (Rev. 13:12)

Summary of the Introduction

Only ONE Church was founded by Christ, not a 'Council of Churches'. That Church must still be in existence today, enjoying His everlasting Promise. Not only must it still be clearly recognisable from the indelible characteristics He gave it: it must by necessity be the only Church which still has the fullness of the unity Christ endowed His Church with. This fullness can never be shared with any other 'church'. Anyone not "in communion" with this unity in Faith, Doctrine, Structure, Government, Sacraments and Tradition is either still outside the Church or else on the way out.

But no one here on earth will ever be outside the influence of this Holy Church...

Chapter One

The Fundamental Practice of the World Council of Churches

Why it is of limited use to recall to contemporary minds that it was the 'ILLUMINATI' who conceived both the idea of One-World Government and the idea of One-World 'Religion', is probably best shown by presenting to people who <u>are</u> interested in these things the following two quotes produced by authors exposed to vastly different backgrounds and experiences.

"I am baffled by the way people still speak of the West as if it were at least a cultural unity against communism. But the West is divided, not only politically, but by an invisible cleavage. On one side are the voiceless masses with their own subdivisions and fractures. On the other side is the enlightened, articulate elite which to one degree or other has rejected the religious roots of the civilization - the roots without which it is no longer Western civilization, but a new order of beliefs, attitudes and mandates. In short, this is the order of which communism is one <u>logical</u> expression. Not originating in Russia, but in the cultural capitals of the West, reaching Russia by clandestine delivery via the old underground centres in Cracow, Vienna, Berne, Zurich and Geneva. It is a WESTERN BODY OF BELIEFS that now threatens the West from RUSSIA. As a body of Western beliefs: secular, materialistic, and rationalistic, the intelligentsia of the West share it, and are therefore always committed to a secret, emotional complicity with communism, of which they dislike, not the communism, but only what, by chance of history, Russia has specially added to it: slave-labour camps, purges, MVD et alia. And that, not because the Western intellectuals find them unjustifiable, but because they are afraid of being caught in them. If they could have communism without the brutalities of overlording that the Russian experience bred, they have only marginal objections. Why should they object? What else is Socialism but Communism with the claws retracted?" [Note: 'retracted', not 'removed'].[3]

Is this not the exact mentality which, according to the already quoted prediction of Pope St. Pius X some 55 years earlier, 'would bring back to the world (Europe!) the reign of legalised cunning and brute force, and the oppression of the weak and of all those who toil and suffer'? For it is EVOLUTION that Whittaker Chambers is talking about here, that Western body of beliefs, born in the West from the peculiarly Western secular, materialistic and rationalistic mind, which found its way to Russia and is now threatening Europe from Russia. ["Russia will spread its errors right around the world!", Our Lady, at FATIMA]. Evolution has taken from the West any ideological weapon against the advancement of Communism intent on depriving the West of its freedom and wealth. For evolution and Christianity are incompatible!

---

[3] Whittaker Chambers. *Cold Friday*. 1964. pp. 225, 226, after his conversion from Communism.

What started centuries ago with NOMINALISM which robbed Western Man of Absolute values, Absolute Truth, and an Absolute Moral Order, which made HIM the measure of all things, and which has not stopped developing since, that, the final product of this whole chain-reaction: modern man, enjoying materialism as never before without a thought for God or conscience, would now love to stop. But stop it he can't. For Western Man is so cynically atheistic that – as we just saw – he is indistinguishable from a communist. And so he will live under Communism WITH THE CLAWS FULLY OUT, be it under another name ...

Is Whittaker Chambers the only shrewd observer of the world political scene who dares to point the finger – in spite of an irrational press – to the very root which caused our world to get <u>in such a mess</u>? Here is the considered opinion of another man who shouts, with equal finality, from the rooftops: 'because evolution has failed miserably'! It has failed man. It has failed the modern scientist, the modernist priest, the Teilhard de Chardin nun, the liberal bishop, the biased college professor, as well as the liberated woman, the marxist social workers, the humanist catechists and teachers, the secular politician.

> "Through means of psychological behaviourism, man is left with nothing that transcends his experiences. He has no values left and no morals, and his life becomes sheer practice without theory. But he consoles himself with the thought that life should be experimental. Modern man feels he should try all ideas since he will acknowledge no basis or yardstick by which to evaluate any idea, except trial and error which is strictly *groping in the dark*, which makes him essentially *an irrational animal let loose in nature*. In net: modern man is pathetically susceptible to making all the mistakes of those who went before him simply because he does not know enough history, enough tested principles, enough religion."[4]

---

[4] Lammerts, as quoted by Dr. John N. Moore, Ed. D., in *Neo-Darwinism and Society*, commenting on Prof. Richard Weaver's book: *Ideas Have Consequences*.

Here we have a description of people without a philosophy worth of that name, i.e. without training in thinking (remember Pope St. Pius X: 'no discipline of the mind'). Contemporaries without a proper foundation on which a supernatural edifice of Faith can be built. "Irrational animals", no longer "chiming in with Revelation".

Only our Twentieth Century contemporaries described to a Tee in these two quotes will believe, and will continue to believe, that a deprivation of intellect on such a gigantic scale is not by design. Only intellects destroyed by Existentialism can be manipulated to believe that such a destruction is a gain. Only a Joan Kirner can truly believe herself, and can make other minds attuned to her wavelength accept, that her annihilation of education in the State of Victoria is the greatest good for youth within the last two thousand years. Only a modernist priest, emaciated on a starvation diet of Truth in Satan's concentration camp, can truly believe, looking out through the wire of his compound, that the true children of the Church he sees enjoying freedom in <u>obedience</u> to Her rule, are behind the barb wire and that he himself is free ...

This explains why the WCC as a product of this western thinking, is capable of believing that its smoke-riddled bowels of total religious anarchy are THE most precious gift the Holy Spirit has reserved for a generation which has lost all appreciation, most of all of itself! Thus, as said before, in order to know that the WCC was 'invented' to destroy the Catholic Faith of millions, and to block the entry into the One True Church of countless other millions, it is highly irrelevant for this generation, and therefore totally unnecessary, to trace the WCC all the way back to Adam Weishaupt and his Illuminati. It is sufficient to quote from its Transatlantic Charter that no member church may lay claim to uniqueness in the sense of considering itself as being 'uniquely founded by Christ'; may not lay claim to the possession of Christ's gift of unity, and may no longer teach doctrines which are not broadly held by all the other member churches.

Thus, to put 'paid' to any lawful belief in the Divinity of Christ, the WCC, as its 1961 World Conference in New Delhi, adopted as its 'christ' the 'Cosmic-Christ': that feverish figment of Teilhard de Chardin's evolutionary imagination ...

That these stipulations make of the Catholic Church 'a maverick church' condemned by the whole WCC is of course by design, which turns the World Council of Churches into a veritable "Synagogue of Satan" (Rev. 2:9). So, even if bishops have formally made whole dioceses members of this Council, individual Catholics 'who prefer to remain in their Father's House' are morally bound to disclaim any part.

This then is the Fundamental Practice of the WCC for its affiliated churches and their members: to impose from above the 'freedom to believe anything or nothing', and to impose on all its members as a condition for admission the obligation to allow any other member church the freedom to believe in anything or nothing as long as no such church believes or preaches what is unique to the Catholic Church on pain of being branded a 'maverick church'.

This makes Modernist Catholics ideal members of the WCC, for Modernist Catholics have long since ceased to believe uniquely what the Holy Catholic Church teaches and believes.

Modernists no longer believe that the Catholic Church teaches infallibly.

They no longer believe that the Catholic Church is unique and can legitimately claim to be exclusively the One True Church founded by Christ for the salvation of everyone.

Modernist Catholics have shown themselves to be quite prepared to drop any teaching which sets the Catholic Church apart from any other 'church'; and to stick to a broad, liberal and 'generic' christianity, the type of amorphous goo the US bishops accused RENEW of spawning.

Modernist Catholics have shown themselves to be ashamed of their Holy Mother, the Catholic Church. They believe in practise that the harlot which aborted their Catholic Faith 'that came to them from the Apostles' is their true and only mother.

So, when Modernist Catholics line up their 'church' for membership of the WCC, they pretend that that take an admittedly RENEWED, but nevertheless authentic 'catholic church' with them into this modern replica of Babel. But, as has become increasingly more clear after years of strenuous but futile efforts, they only manage to chase their own evolutionary tail in affiliating their man-made contraption to this One-World 'Church'.

That this stranglehold of Modernism is real, and that the Modernists recognise a threat against their own 'fundamental practise' of only allowing to be taught what they hold themselves, can easily be gleaned from the punishment that is meted out to anyone who publicly opposes them. Not even bishops fighting for orthodoxy in seminaries and Catholic schools are spared public ridicule and a veritable 'war of attrition'. Long before Antichrist has made his appearance, it is already 'a matter of life and death'...

Summary of Chapter One

Not only is it impossible for the WCC to be the Church founded by Christ: the Council is in fundamental error in pretending that it is complying with Christ's wish in searching for an as yet non-existing unity. The WCC is on a collision course with the Holy Spirit on two (2) counts:

(a) in stipulating that no member 'church' may claim to possess the unity of Christ's Church, let alone claim to enjoy that possession exclusively, as the Holy Catholic Church does; and

(b) by forbidding any member 'church' to hold or teach what follows immediately from this claim of full possession of this exclusive unity: the dogmas of the Holy Roman Church. No one can truly believe to have inherited from Christ the 'right' to lay down that only that may be taught which is common to all denominations, as such a claim has no foundation in Revealed Truth. This peace-at-any-price in 'religion' is Antichrist's pre-requisite for peace-at-any-price in politics. Catholics who claim to believe strongly in what sets the Holy Catholic Church apart from any other 'church', will be denied the glory of being persecuted for their Catholic Faith. They will be haunted for being a menace to the political unity of the world with their 'maverick' Faith ...

Chapter Two

The Fundamental Doctrine of the World Council of Churches

What firmly held conviction must lie at the root of the 'fundamental practice' discussed in the previous chapter?

What is the ONE secret that sometimes gives to the eyes of 'born again' Christians that far-away gleam as if they are already fixed on Paradise, but more often than not gives those eyes an expression that exposes the inner fanaticism associated with this secret?

Whence the strength of that unknown force shared by all the Modernists that will catapult them through the sound barrier into a strange trajectory that seems to hold them captive in perpetuity by the attraction of some unholy fascination? What makes them enter the slippery slide of believing the opposite of what the Holy Catholic Church has taught with perennial unanimity still convinced they believe in the same 'church'?

What will make a priest ruin the Holy Sacrifice of the Mass, and will make a woman go on the pill, in the firm conviction that all who oppose the use they make of their newly-found freedom have lost touch with the Catholic Church?

What makes a nun advocate abortion and a priest advocate the abolition of the papacy over national TV and radio? What makes Catholic teachers vote in workshops of Catholic education conferences for the abolition of the Hierarchical Church because this 'outmoded model' opposes women-priests, married clergy and gay and contraceptive lifestyles?

Yes, what is the <u>one</u> answer to all these questions? What is the name of this inner conviction, this fascination? By what name must this gravitational force be identified, that keeps so many in strange orbits by a new attraction, ostensibly more appreciated than the one exerted by Our Lord in the Blessed Sacrament, discarded as one of those 'maverick' doctrines no longer allowed to be held or taught in the newly-founded 'church' of the false ecumenism?

Chapter Two: The Fundamental Doctrine of the WCC

What has been that 'blinding flash of inspiration' in which Satan has transformed himself 'as an angel of light' to 'modern man', that pathetic end-product of a faked evolution? If indeed evolution has more to do with this new fascination than Divine Revelation, around which planet, then, is the whole World Council of Churches and the whole Modernist movement held in orbit, helplessly, as if by invisible strings? If it is a 'planet' discovered by 'Evolution', then it can only be the true 'Planet of the Apes', a 'planet', that is, of do-as-you-go-along, of endless imitations and improvisations (Lammerts); an imaginary planet found by a pseudo-science to feed a truly false 'religion', The 'planet' of the 'Cosmic Christ'.

Here it is the appropriate time and place to firmly impress on my readers how far removed I am from casting any slur on any individual effort made daily by members of the human race to lift their souls to God. With my Divine Master and my Holy Mother the Catholic Church, I have great compassion with any Samaritan woman at any well anywhere in the world, or with any sinner crucified on the cross of his own making. But what is being singled out here for severe castigation and held aloft for global condemnation, is precisely the same thing for which Our Blessed Lord reserved His harshest words and His most severe indictment:

> "Alas for you, scribes and Pharisees, you hypocrites! You who shut up the Kingdom of Heaven in men's faces, neither going in yourselves nor allowing others to go in who want to." (Mt. 23:13).

> "A lawyer then spoke up. 'Master', he said, 'when you speak like this you insult us too'. 'Alas for you, lawyers also', He replied ... 'You have taken away the key of knowledge. You have not gone in yourselves and have prevented others going in who wanted to'." (Lk. 11:45, 52).

> "You will die in your sin!" (Jo. 8:21, 24).

What was at stake then, in the days of Our Lord, to deserve this clearest of warnings, is still very much at stake here and now. It is now, as it was then, the ORGANISED effort, imposed from above: to keep away from Revelation any 'Samaritan woman at any well of the world'. Here and now we are not dealing with adherents of strange religions: we are dealing with the organised effort of the Modernists and the World Council of Churches to keep the peoples of the world away from the Catholic Church, and to gather them all into a kind of man-made structure where they are allowed to believe what they like as long as it is NOT Revealed Truth, as held up by the Catholic Church for the salvation of mankind. And in the chaos that must inevitably follow the forced captivity in such stifling surroundings, the 'key of knowledge' has been conveniently lost ….

And now the ONE answer to the queries with which we started this second chapter is staring us in the face.

Now we understand the deadly incantations the witches were chanting while brewing the potions of 'the great apostasy', not only on the moors of England, but precisely in the 'dark workshops' of the fatal congresses of the WCC from 1961 onwards: New Delhi, Uppsala, Bangkok, Kyoto, Louvain,

Canberra, and ever since. When we read the proceedings of these great world gatherings, we see the dried-up stains left by the spilled potions drunk at these assemblies by ex- and non-Catholic members in attendance; mute testimonies to the fundamental switch.

And the 'Cosmic Christ' of New Delhi in 1961 is the biggest spill of them all, a religious oil-slick of such formidable proportions that it has gone right around the world with devastating effect. Its giveaway message is so clear that it cannot possibly be misread or misunderstood. And this same message, this same fundamental switch, lies expressed in the garbled versions of 'sermons' preached by priests who desperately want to "look like the Lamb", but who inwardly have become so mesmerised by the new siren song of freedom and liberation that, according to St. John, they "speak like the Dragon".

And what is this glittering promise? What is this cherished lolly, so sticky that it is impossible to remove it from the hands of those who clutch it? The one card on which every Modernist has staked his or her eternal salvation? The ONE doctrine that must be right, or else the world-wide revolt against a

2000-year old Church has been in vain? The one last antidote wayward bishops, priests, nuns, catechists, theologians and teachers hope will commute Our Lord's final death sentence: "You will die in your sins" to an ineffectual censure?

It is the suicidal concept 'that salvation is inevitable'. That salvation is secured. That the victory won by Christ over sin and death is so certain that we can safely forget to work for our own eternal salvation and that of our fellow-man, and to use this newly-discovered 'freedom' so gained to switch instead to an earthly 'salvation' from poverty, hunger and want, from oppression and every kind of disease, and from any political obstruction. But since that proves to be an impossible task if it is not undertaken by the heroic sacrifices demanded by the new Law of Love proclaimed on Calvary, the reality of this newly-found freedom very quickly degenerates to the selfish mandate 'to do as we please', and to guard ourselves against every kind of want.

It is this fatal switch of which the witches were chanting, the one which transfers the universal Redemption won by Christ for all mankind, (which makes individual Salvation possible ON CONDI-

TION) to an inevitable universal Salvation, which would result in making the individual salvation unconditional and absolute. It was for this reason that 'evolution' was laid at the foundation of the notorious *Dutch Catechism,* and that it was forcibly introduced into every Catholic school, when the discredited doctrine was being discarded in ever-widening scientific circles. For 'Teilhardian evolution' ends up inevitably in 'God-Omega'. We all are the 'Teilhardian evolution', and the 'Teilhardian evolution' is the 'Cosmic Christ', and so, as the 'Cosmic-Christ', we end up inevitably in 'God-Omega'…. What a tarot card upon which to bank one's eternal salvation!

Thus it has come about that the World Council of Churches has turned itself into a huge 'salvation club' with a fully paid-up membership, whose members have time on their hands to please themselves on the jolly cruise ship bound for eternity. And the Modernists have taken over this 'salvation cry', chanting everywhere in unison with the WCC: 'We are the Covenant people'. 'We can't go wrong'. 'Our salvation is secured'. 'The old Church was severely mistaken on this point'….

But what did Our Lord tell the startled Jews when they tried that same tactic on Him, that same direct rebuttal on Him: 'We have Abraham for our father', as the reason why they should no longer have to listen to Him? This is what He said:

"You have the devil for your father. You will die in your sins". (John 8:44).

His universal Redemption, which included all the Jews, did NOT turn out to be an inevitable salvation for these Jews! So, on Divine Authority, it is truly possible for redeemed people to die in their sins and to lose their eternal salvation.

And with this, with this colossal switch and their unholy conviction, the Modernists have truly embraced what Pope St. Pius X singled out as being "the synthesis of all heresies". For the 'fathers of all heresies', the two most ancient heresies known to the Church, *Gnosticism* and *Manichaeism*, both have at their root a dual system: the 'doctrine' that next to the Catholic Church there exists a 'parallel' or 'dual' system of 'salvation', which will inevitably end up in what was in their days the equivalent of 'god-omega', but along a much easier road. And millions who have believed this message and who have shaken off the Cross, and have taken the easier road, either have perished or will perish. For all this is not different from the Jews who had severe difficulties accepting Our Lord's teaching and sought refuge in the untenable creed that being a descendant from Abraham would prove to be a safe, 'parallel system'. There is nothing 'automatic' on the human road to eternity ....

So now that we have isolated the fundamental misconception of the WCC and its Modernist supporters, we can see quite clearly how perfectly this fits in with their fundamental practice described in Chapter One.

If one's salvation is secured; if everyone 'goes to heaven' along his or her own path; if therefore we can put a moratorium on out-dated missionary activities; and instead leave the peoples of the world safely in their cultures and beliefs (which was the almost unanimous vote of the WCC's World Congress on Missions at Bangkok in 1973); to direct our concerns to the political and social arena, liberating people from 'oppressive dogmas' and systems, if necessary with the aid of force, and even with force of arms (Tutu): all different expressions of the same fundamental 'doctrine', then it follows quite logically for the WCC and their Modernist allies to embark on their fundamental practice: have nothing to do with the pre-Vatican II Catholic Church nor with its post-Conciliar remnants. For this Church had somehow lost this exhilarating doctrine of the universality of individual salvation.

But some 1900 years ago God's Providence had placed a guard, 'an Angel with a flaming sword', at the entrance of His Church, His glorious New Paradise, to protect Her decisively against any inroads that this hellish doctrine, *that the road to Hell no longer exists,* was intended to make within Her walls. This 'doctrine', together with all who took it up, is strictly for what is on the outside, for those who wish to be damned. Even if preached in the Sanctuaries of the Holy Catholic Church, or in 'catholic' schools and 'seminaries', it will never be part of that Church; it will never deceive "those whose names are written in the Book of Life". (Phil. 4:3; Rev. 3:5; 13:8; 17:8; 20:12, 13; 21: 27; 22:19).

When in his visions on the island of Patmos, St. John saw a religious monstrosity roaming the world towards the latter days, trying desperately "to look like the Lamb", he gave it the only name that describes it accurately: he called it "a beast", "the second beast". That this beast is anything but 'religious', St. John makes clear when he gives us a description of its activities; and no one but the Holy Spirit could sum those activities so succinctly for us as His holy author did under His direct inspiration: "This second beast does everything in its power to subjugate the whole world to the tyranny of the first beast". In other words, the second beast is nothing but the 'religious' arm of Antichrist, a political monster. A uniform, tolerant 'One-World Religion' will facilitate the political unity under One-World government. And any Catholic opposing this tolerant, one-world, ecumenical and political 'religion', will not be persecuted for his religious beliefs: he or she will be persecuted for disrupting the one-world political unity with his or her 'maverick' doctrines which are no longer held by the mainstream of 'christianity'.

Armed with these insights, first with regard to the practical attitude of the World Council of Churches and Modernist Catholics viz-a-viz the Roman Catholic Church, and second with regard to the fundamental doctrine which both camps have made their own to underpin their strong aversion for the pre-Vatican II Church, the stage is now set to ascertain if St. John's description of "the second beast" fits both the WCC and its twin-collaborator, the Modernist 'church'.

Summary of Chapter Two

To be in open contradiction with Revealed Truth, and to make decisions as if Revealed Truth does not exist, means finding oneself on a collision course with the Holy Spirit according to the condemnation of St. Paul in 2 Thess. 2:10, "they did not possess the love of Truth which could have saved them". No one can ever claim to embark on a collision course with Truth 'out of love of Christ' Who calls Himself the Truth. We may now also quote Pope St. Pius X in support of St. Paul here, when he declared that such practices must be considered to be part of "the great movement of apostasy".

The leadership of the WCC tells lies when it maintains that the practice on which it has embarked is not on a collision course with Revealed

Truth, and is not displeasing to the Holy Spirit. With St. Paul they know that: (i) 'Love of Truth' rejects syncretism; (ii) 'Love of Truth' rejects the idea that 'one faith is as good as another'; (iii) 'Love of Truth' rejects as false any elaborate set-up of being dead-set against the pre-Conciliar Catholic Church in the hope that the 'church of Modernism' is the real one, the RENEWed post-Vatican II Church they can get along with fine. They know that all this requires that one does not look too closely! Somehow they must have stumbled on a 'fundamental conviction' in support of their evil practice of not being 'in love with Truth', yet somehow thinking it does not matter, that it does not put them on the road to Hell, but that on the contrary 'it will save them'.

The search for the diabolical foundation on which the WCC's conviction is based "that one does not have to be in love with Revealed Truth" in order to be 'saved' only comes to an end, when we come face to face with the same 'foundation' on which Modernism is built: the belief 'that the road to Hell no longer exists'.

In other words, their fundamental doctrine is that salvation is INEVITABLE. That salvation is guaranteed no matter what road one is on. "Don't worry about Hell. Join the salvation club and become a fully paid-up member as quickly as possible. For it is only after that that you can safely believe, or do, what you like. Only do not get yourselves mixed up with what the Holy Roman Catholic Church proposes for belief! That is only 'maverick'. Just stick to what WE tell you is 'catholic'."

Chapter Three

The World Council of Churches and the "Everlasting Enmity"

In 1963 a group of Protestant evangelical bible scholars produced a little pamphlet entitled "THE COMING WORLD CHURCH", of which by 1974 well over 100,000 copies had been sold. In this study these scholars turned the spotlight on the World Council of Churches and its relentless ecumenical drive, because they felt threatened by it. Although subsequent analyses by protestant theologians, notably the scholarly documentation (an eyewitness account) by Prof. Dr. Peter Beyerhaus: "Bangkok '73", have gained in comprehensiveness and depth, the work of these authors stands out if only because all the follow-up work corroborated rather than corrected their accurate 'first approximation'.

The timing of the documentation is of some significance. By 1963 VATICAN II was still two years away from closing its historic debates, when, amidst a host of other issues, the Catholic attitude on unity and ecumenism were still in the formative stages. But by then the World Council of Churches had already two years since its 1961 World Congress in New Delhi, adopted the 'Cosmic Christ' as the 'centre' around which all its future religious endeavours would become meaningful.

The main thesis of these biblical scholars is, that the WCC is so honey-combed with liberal Protestantism, that biblical truth and revealed faith are traded off in favour of the formation of an organisation which, because of its two main requirements: that it be world-wide and smoothly run, by essence must embrace syncretism.

This is an accurate observation. In order that the Marxist tool can be an effective instrument for its true objective: One-World Government, it must be just as tightly run, and be just as secular, as the global ends which are envisaged. To speed up the smooth transition from 'religious' to 'secular', and to help in the acceptance of this syncretism as 'coming from the Holy Spirit', the magic word 'ecumenism' is being overused. That, and of course the word 'love'.

Chapter Three: The WCC and the "Everlasting Enmity" 45

To support their claim that the WCC is no longer orthodox Protestant, the authors endeavour to show *inter alia* that the WCC is becoming ... catholic! At first glance this may appear such an unexpected twist, that, this proposition warrants further investigation. And even if this reveals, as e.g. on p.50, that the authors still adhere to the Reformation doctrine of equating the Catholic Church with the 'scarlet woman of the Apocalypse' – and so by association view the WCC as part of this abomination, because it is the only one they know – a Catholic reader must not lose interest at this stage just because of that, thinking mistakenly that this is all the authors have to say about the 'catholicity' of the WCC. But it is time they are allowed to speak for themselves.

> "A definite Catholic pattern is now beginning to shape up in the World Council. With evangelical Protestant churches in a decisive minority, SACRAMENTARIAN and LITURGICAL churches (my stress) predominate in the Secretariate, the Central Committee and the Divisions and Commis-

sions. The Eastern Orthodox Churches, the Coptic, Armenian, Syrian, Anglican, and many of the newly created 'younger churches' are definitely Catholic. Add to these the European State churches, the American Episcopal, Lutheran, Presbyterian, and Methodist churches, which are increasingly 'high church' in their practice."

"The situation is clear. In conferences and study groups dealing with the nature of the 'coming great church', the Catholic ecumenical pattern as respects its ministry. Its policy, its worship, its sacraments, its witness and its view of salvation is definitely favoured over the evangelical Protestant position."

It becomes obvious from this extract that here a very careful study of word meanings is called for, since THE Catholic Church is not a member of the World Council of Churches, and never will be, and so can never be responsible for its directions. 'Catholic' here means what most Protestant churches see as a defect in The True Catholic Church: its preoccupation with SACRAMENTS and LITURGY over witness. For Catholics this is not a problem as they see in the Seven Sacraments instituted by Christ not only signs of the graces they signify, but actual instruments of those graces, which is rejected by Reformed Churches.

To them Catholics are preoccupied with meaningless rites and empty rituals at the expense of witness, which of course is precisely what was taking place, according to this document, as early as 1961 in the WCC, and has continued ever since, until now in 1991 we can testify to the complete absence of any witness of Apostolic Tradition, as behooves a syncretist tool in the hand of the One-Worlders. Seen in this light, the observation made here is very astute! As already remarked, the Catholic sacramental, liturgical, and salvation doctrine is bad enough to swallow for these evangelical Protestants, but that does not prevent them from being observant enough to see clearly the radical changes that are needed in Modernist Catholics when, in seeking full-blown membership in the WCC, they pretend to take the Catholic Church with them in their nose dive to annihilation ...

I will now quote from two places in their book where these authors have shown to understand what is at stake.

1. Dr. G. Bromley Oxnam's book "On the Rock" (p. 15 sq).

"Dr. G. Bromley Oxnam is credited with having prepared the blueprints for both the National Council of Churches (USA) and the WCC. He thoroughly understood the role they would play in achieving his dream of 'The Coming Great Church'."

[Now listen here on what that 'dream' is based]

"In his book "On the Rock", this late great ecumenist bypassed all the basic tenets of evangelical Christian doctrine, and called for the abandonment of all traditional and organizational barriers to church union. He proposed first to bring about inclusive cooperative Protestant action in the realm of church functions. Next he would create an ecumenical ministry. The bishop himself said he would be gladly re-ordained under this system. He declared:

'I would gladly kneel in a service of mutual sharing in which the blessings of the different ordinations might be *symbolically* conferred upon me'."

"Then Oxnam enlarges the picture:

'United actions in many fields would follow ... missions ... education ... united theological seminaries ... the ministers of the church ... The union of American christianity would electrify the world and accelerate the trend towards union in every continent.

'Finally' said the bishop, 'it will be possible to kneel before a common altar with the Roman Catholic Church, beg forgiveness of the Christ for disunity and sharing the bread and wine of holy communion, rise in his

Spirit to form the Holy Catholic Church to which all Christians may belong'."

If this enforced participation of the Holy Catholic Church in the religious disintegration through the envisaged anarchy of the One-World church's 'salvation' is the theory, then (still quoting from the same book) *what is the practice*?

"The Northern California Council of Churches will make a good example. In America this ecumenical church is being built through the actions of Councils affiliated with the National Council of Churches, and in mergers of various denominations. A local Council has what is known as a *Comity Committee* which assigns certain territories to certain denominations *to the exclusion of all others.* Before any new church can be established, a permit must first be secured (*coercion*) from the local Council of Churches. City planning commissions and even national housing administrators are advised that *maverick churches*, that is, those that do not bear the stamp of Council approval, should not be allowed to construct buildings in areas under their control.

All pastors of Churches which received a 'permit' and have been allocated specific territories by the Comity Commission, are advised that they represent not only their own denomination BUT ALSO THE ECUMENICAL CHURCH. They are required TO EMPHASISE THE TEACHINGS WHICH THEIR DENOMINATIONS SHARE WITH THE REST OF CHRISTENDOM. (My stress.)

In other words, the 'Ecumenical Church' already exists in the thinking of the World Council of Churches, as does an 'Ecumenical Ministry', with all planning for the future motivated by a determination to achieve ONE CHURCH FOR ONE WORLD."

This leaves in clarity as with regard to both theory and practice nothing to be desired.

It is becoming pretty obvious that the Catholic Church who will not go along with this sort of ecumenism, will be considered a 'maverick church' by the unanimous decision of all the churches and councils who DO go along with it.

Does this give us some idea of the size of the slice which at the moment is in the process of separating itself from the Catholic Church, after having adopted teachings alien to Her Tradition, but in conformity with the demands of this false ecumenism? There can be no doubt that in the Eyes of God this separating slice is the 'maverick church'. But for the Bride of the Lamb of God to be called by that name here on earth in the not too distant future, She must, as the deserted Mother, have been left behind as the numerical 'minority', just as Her adorable Head once had been on Calvary.

Chapter Interlude: Hans Kung

The foregoing proves conclusively that the big Catholic slice which will go along with this 'ecumenism', keeping up the pretence that it controls the Catholic Church in this amalgamation, will have to emphasise the teachings on the Sacraments, the Eucharist, the Pope and Infallibility, and on Our

Blessed Lady, which are shared with all the other ecumenical denominations and the rest of 'christendom'. This means that strong demands will be made on Catholics to adopt a 'theology' which will abolish Transubstantiation; which will rob the Sacraments of their ontological, Supernatural reality; which will make a figurehead of the Pope, leaving effective control in the hands of a democratically constituted government; and which will rob Our Lord and Saviour Jesus Christ of His Divinity, and His Holy Mother of Her Divine Maternity, to make them both better fit in with the 'Cosmic Christ' of 'evolution'. Since this is the only philosophy, theology, catechesis and exegesis in any Catholic institute of higher and lower learning tolerated in the West, we Catholics can cease wondering about the size of the slice which is in the process of separating itself from the Catholic Church in preparation for initiation into the cosmic ecumenical phenomenon.

And this very active slice has for its able pioneer none other than the celebrated daredevil HANS KUNG. That this man is a heretic, no one who kept the priceless gift of his or her supernatural, infused, divine and Catholic Faith can deny. That his heresies are enthusiastically received by millions, are multiplied over and over again, and are hailed as the true expression of twentieth-century 'catholicism' cannot be denied either. He is the ultimate in subversion. His call-to-arms for ecumenism are unmistakably calls to apostasy. One that springs to mind was the one contained in his paper which he delivered at a conference of 'theologians' at the University of Notre Dame in 1977. In this he urged all Catholics and Protestants to openly protest for ecumenical union by starting grassroot inter-communion in defiance of Pope and bishops, so as to force the great reunion through.

And he was not alone in his call. Fr. Eugene KENNEDY S.J. of Chicago Loyola University urged all Catholics to the same disobedience. "You just make changes in the grassroots. Changes have the habit of coming to be accepted ..."

Subsequent conventions, advertisements and petitions by hundreds of 'catholic' philosophers and theologians have made the break with the Catholic Church all but final ...

Who was it again who once wrote with the authority of the Holy Spirit Himself about the religious monstrosity "that it would do everything in its power to subjugate the whole world to the tyranny of the first beast"?

2. The BLAKE proposal (p. 15 sqq).

Hans Kung's ravings (the word was used by Pope St. Pius X in *Pascendi* to describe the utterances of the Modernists) are not new or even original. Dr. Eugene CARSON BLAKE envisages a new church which would combine the best elements of Catholic beauty ('Is that all?'), reformed theology and evangelical fervour. It would claim and manifest its historic continuity with the church before and after the Reformation; accept consecration of all its bishops and presbyters in the 'apostolic succession'; express belief in the Holy Trinity; administer TWO SACRAMENTS; and include a wide variety and diversity in doctrinal beliefs and forms of worship. The Bible and historic creeds of christendom would be acceptable, BUT ONLY AS SYMBOLIC STATEMENTS of great truths which are being better understood with the 'evolution of christendom'.

There have grown up world-wide confessional organisations to put the 'Blake proposal' into effect: The Lutheran World Federation; the World Methodist Council; the Baptist World Alliance; the International Congregational Church; the Alliance of Reformed Churches throughout the world, holding to the Presbyterian System; the World Convention of Churches of Christ; the Lambeth Conference of Bishops of the Anglican Communion; and the eastern Orthodox Episcopate. All of these have significant relations with the WCC and hold regularly scheduled World Conferences, in which all participate UNDER WCC LEADERSHIP.

Furthermore, there is the International Missionary Council, which emerged with the World Council of Churches at the 1961 New Delhi Assembly, which adopted the idea of the 'cosmic-christ', showing the unmistakable fingerprint of the 'mastermind'.

WCC representatives are furnishing the leadership to establish an 'All-Africa' Conference; a Latin America Conference; and the Near-East Christian Council. Eventually the whole world will be organised and be receiving guidance, and even control, from Geneva through the Regional Councils.

[So far the summarised relevant part of the authors of "The Coming World Church".]

[Who was it who once wrote under infallible inspiration: "And the whole world will be running after the Beast?"]

Could anyone believe, or even seriously consider, the proposition that, for the first time in history, 'Ideas would NOT have Consequence'? And that global ideas such as described here, would NOT result in global consequences? That against the rising tidal wave of such infidelity, cowardice and determination, our Holy Mother the Catholic Church will NOT end up being branded a 'maverick church'? Not that this universal desertion would in any way affect this wonderful Church, or would spell its end. It will only spell the end of the traitors.

You see, the World Council of Churches, not being founded by Christ, and not enjoying 'a perennial youth' in the absence of the Divine Promise of perpetuity, must (as the astute authors just quoted observed with such great perspicacity and logic) be of its very nature SYNCRETISTIC in order to have some hope of survival by its own power. But that means two things (1) this 'Church of the New Age' does NOT come from the Holy Spirit; and (2) that it carries inevitably and by its very nature the seeds of its own destruction within itself, no matter what brave face all those priests, nuns and teachers 'who still try to look like the Lamb and hide the fact that they speak like the Dragon' put on their cowardice, when their outward behaviour shows that they are at home in this new 'brotherhood'.

But the Holy Catholic Church does enjoy with an inner glow and with great gratitude to God 'Her perennial youth' (Pope John XXIII). As the sole Church founded by Christ, She is unique. And because she is alone, and alone enjoys the promise of immortality and the promise by Her Founder of Her everlasting integrity, She is also the only Church who inherited 'the Everlasting Enmity' pronounced in Paradise 'between the Woman and Her Seed' and 'you and your seed'. Only a Church who carries 'These Everlasting Promises' can afford to stick forever to an unpopular Faith and the unpopular teachings 'that came to Her from the Apostles', and to carry these unhurriedly and infallibly through the two thousand years of Her great Tradition. She is the only Church who can afford the luxury of not changing Her timeless message nor to speak with the voice of the world 'in order to be heard', since She does not have to be popular in order to survive. She will survive in spite of the world, and so save the world. She is the only Church in the whole wide world who does not have to worry about Her numerical strength or Her prestige, or about standing with the great and influential of this earth in order to be influential Herself.

This Holy Church will never be under the control of evil nor under the command of men. She can live under any system, outlast any enemy, survive any death. For the Church, THE Church, does not rest on human counsels nor on the councils of creatures here below. Her Head is divine, so is Her Life. Within Her is the pearl of great beauty for which any merchant-in-the-know is prepared to sacrifice everything in order to possess it: an unchanging Catholic Faith, the most priceless gift of Almighty God to finite little man. And that is the reason why those who show to be more at home in the brotherhood of the World Council of Churches and more attuned to its garbled message, will lose this priceless pearl of great beauty, will lose their Catholic Faith, because they were not prepared to SACRIFICE everything for it! They have no root in them, they do not last. "Let some trial come, some persecution on account of the Word, and they fall away at once".

For it so happens that there does NOT exist "a no-man's land": a piece of neutral ground or 'peaceful coexistence' in between the forces of 'The Everlasting Enmity'.

Summary of Chapter Three

Non-Catholic accusations levelled against the WCC taken from its official records are telling. The few quoted here show, that even Protestants see the WCC as SYNCRETISTIC, that is, picking out what it likes from anywhere (not necessarily from religion) as long as it is bland enough to blend. A real patch-up job.

In no longer being concerned if a proposition is true or not, and certainly not being concerned if it is Revealed Truth, the WCC is fighting the Holy Catholic Church. NOT the RENEWED ONE, as it is being paraded everywhere 'as coming to us from the Modernists'; but the One that has been handed down to us 'as She came to us from the Apostles'. And in being on a war-footing with the HOLY Roman Catholic Church, the WCC shows itself to be on the wrong side of the 'everlasting enmity' established by God in Paradise. And it is highly significant to bring out in this context of global warfare, that the only opponent identified by God in the 'Everlasting Enmity' against the 'Woman of Genesis' is Satan: "you and your seed".

Global ideas, translated into such far-reaching instructions, must of necessity have world-wide consequences. The most important repercussion is that, by pretending to be 'Christ-like', the WCC lays itself wide open to the charge of being 'the second beast of the Book of Revelation': a global religious monstrosity, forerunner of Antichrist, which St. John describes as 'trying desperately to look like the Lamb, but in reality mouths the Dragon's message'.

Which message? The lie that personal salvation s guaranteed and won! 'The Christ' did everything for us, so now we can forget about him. All he expects us to do now 'in his name' is to free the world from political oppression, poverty and sickness by supplying lots of cash and of course free arms, contraceptives, condoms and abortion-on-demand: all the essential ingredients of the new earthly paradise ...

Chapter Four

"... And with the Increase in Lawlessness, The Love of Many Shall Grow Cold" (Mt. 24:12)

No matter how many Catholics are messing around with the WCC outside the Church, or with Modernism, its twin evil within, thinking them to be acceptable tools in the search for christian unity, closer examination will invariably reveal both ARE ON THE WRONG SIDE OF THE "EVERLASTING ENMITY", and so cannot be genuine instruments in the hands of the Holy Spirit, Who works exclusively through the Catholic Church. Although this great Truth is the unanimous teaching of 2000 years of Catholic Tradition, reinforced by Vatican II and upheld in subsequent encyclicals, it is hotly denied by all the Modernists who want us to believe that the Holy Spirit works exclusively through the ramifications of their 'parallel magisterium', their 'dual system', condemned by a Pope and Saint as "the synthesis of all heresies".

When Satan transforms himself into an 'angel of light' with the aid of his modernist seed, i.e. when light: 'christian language' is being used for fraud, for the creation of ever more darkness and confusion, then ascribing this 'light', this fraudulent use being made of christian terms for the spread of 'the message of the Dragon', to the action of the Holy Spirit, becomes a "Sin against the Light", a blasphemy against the Holy Spirit, which will elude forgiveness in this life and the next. There's is a cold, deliberate and calculated transaction, like Judas Iscariot's, showing the Modernists to be cold-blooded and dead. But what does Scripture say about the position in between the two extremes.

> "I know all about you, how you are neither cold nor hot. I wish you were one or the other, but since you are neither hot nor cold, I am beginning to vomit you out of my mouth." (Rev. 3:15-16)

Nowhere has the sudden cooling effect of this universal lawlessness on genuine love been more devastating than in 'good' priests. Except for a glorious few, <u>many</u> of them (the word used by Our Lord) seem to have grown cold towards the Holy Catholic Church. They are no longer openly and unashamedly in love with Her: their love affair with Her has come to an end, with painful consequences.

They become irritable when they have to defend Her strong doctrines. They are apologetic for Her rightful claim to uniqueness. They are silent in public on Her uncompromising Truths, and they become annoyed when people bring these things up, even in private. They are uncomfortable with the Catholic Church, as uncomfortable as any man in the presence of those who can expose his cowardice and the steps he took to hide it.

And so the blaming starts. When people are genuinely disgusted over the behaviour of children at children's Masses, then they are cast in the role of the Pharisees. When some people are still alarmed over the abyss of ignorance of the Catholic Faith by young and even older children attending 'catholic schools', they are 'judged' themselves and dismissed as judgemental; not only by the Modernists but by good Parish Priests! When with great difficulty, and with great harm to their good name and standing,

Catholics hold up the teachings of the Church and defend Her right to be heard, they are ignored and word is spread around 'that they are pre-Vatican II, that they object to all the changes in the Church and so do not understands them'. And <u>many</u> good priests (the word is used by Christ) go along with that 'to keep the peace' and will <u>not</u> speak out in defence of these children of the Church. Love has cooled off and for their own peace of mind even good pastors are now accepting that such people have only themselves to blame!

But not only is all behaviour studiously avoided 'which is bound to infuriate the Modernists', 'good' pulpits too avoid the mention and the proper development of doctrines that also could cause a stir. And if some of it is very occasionally briefly touched upon, it is treated so apologetically, that people, left tranquilly in their sins after years of such half-heartedness, can read between the lines and dismiss it speedily from their minds.

And so it is possible to hear in all seriousness even from 'good' pulpits "that the Catholic Church has no answer to the mystery of suffering"; that "God does not punish sin" (in flagrant contradiction of Scripture, proper catechetics and human history); "that the Bible is so conditioned by the times in which it was written, that it is now open for almost any interpretations", and "that the love of God is so great that He will save us in spite of our unwillingness", etc.

Although this skating on the thin ice of liberalism may not be straight-out Modernism, even if Modernists hold to it themselves and like to hear it come from priests known for their orthodoxy, it does show that priests who believe in 'peaceful coexistence' with the forces of the 'Everlasting Enmity', and who have set up camp in the mythical 'no-man's land' in between these two forces, are not bowing to the demands of Orthodoxy, but are in reality capitulating to the demands of Modernism. Their uneasiness with unpopular Catholics outspoken in their orthodoxy is further proof that this 'mythical no-man's land' does not exist and that their refuge in it must be classed as a cop-out. With their keenness for the true Catholic position severely blunted, they may, by degrees, have compromised themselves too much and for too long to recognise the occasion when something as innocuous as 'the last straw' finally demands from them, before God, an heroic stand.

According to the invaluable testimony of Pope St. Pius X, the hallmark of our times is indeed that the lawlessness recognised by Christ is abounding, and that the love of many for their glorious Mother, the Catholic Church, has grown cold. When the chips are down they refuse to stand up in their lukewarm state and be counted among the strong defenders of this Church's timeless Truths. And the final irony is that both Orthodox and Modernists are aware that such priests and the Catholics like them are weak and can be relied upon not to rock the boat in the prevailing tide. It is for this reason that they refuse to study RENEW, or the proliferation of advertised courses, for fear of finding enough evidence there to warn the people against them. But when other Catholics provide this service for them, then their evidence is dismissed as untrustworthy, accused of being coloured by bias.

Maybe the foregoing is as good an introduction to what is to come next as any. Pope St. Pius X did more than just draw our attention to the general lawlessness spoken of by Christ: he gave it a name when he called it "the great movement of apostasy organised in every country for the establishment of a One-World Church". This forces us to have a look at a remarkable saying of Our Lord when, in the twenty-first chapter of St. Luke, Our Saviour is being quoted as having said:

> "Jerusalem will be trampled underfoot by the Gentiles until the times of the Gentiles have come to a close." (Lk. 21:24).

Thus, according to Our Blessed Saviour, the Gentiles have only been allotted 'a certain time' in which to enter the Church. After that, it will be the Jews to whom the same opportunity will be given. According to this, it is of the utmost importance for the 'Gentiles' who could have been inside the Church TO BE inside Her saving walls "when the times of the Gentiles have come to a close". For if they are found camping in that 'no-man's land' between the two warring forces at the, for them, most critical period of salvation history, they find themselves outside the Church at the very time 'when the time of the Gentiles have come to an end'. And like the foolish virgins who also were not where they should have been, they too will be banging in vain on the door of the Church: "Lord, Lord open up to us!" "Those who wish to save their lives will lose it."

For the times of the Gentiles to have come truly to an end, and to have come to an end in such a way that it can be pointed out, and can be verified, three conditions must be fulfilled.

1. It must have been foretold, and been foretold in context, so that, once the context has been identified as having occurred, the fulfilment of the prophecy is deemed to be with us too.
2. One must be able to point to a reversal of the influx, i.e. one must be able to recognise an exodus.
3. There must be a receptacle waiting to receive the outflow.

Of the first, there can be no doubt that in the divine Mind only a certain timespan has been allotted to the Gentiles, the non-Jews, "to enter the Kingdom of God", and that this timespan was not arbitrarily chosen by Infinite Perfection, but was – as has always been the case in human history – conditioned by something within the power of the Gentiles themselves: "their return to a state of unbelievable lawlessness coinciding with the cooling off of their original love".

This means that the main context in which Our Lord in the Gospel of St. Luke could predict "the end of the times of the Gentiles, was His foreknowledge and prediction in the Gospel of St. Matthew "that the Gentiles would one day return to a state of complete religious anarchy". The Revolt, coinciding with a loss of love even in good priests, is now clearly upon us, putting for all of us 'the end of the times of the Gentiles' in the broad but accurate context of a 'first approximation'.

St. Paul – whom we shortly will quote with great precision in this whole matter – also links a complete breakdown in religion and morals <u>with a loss of love</u> prior to the appearance of Antichrist. In his Second Letter to the Thessalonians, the second chapter, this great Apostle of the Gentiles writes:

> "But when the Rebel comes, Satan will set to work. There will be all kinds of ... evil, deceiving those who are bound for destruction, BECAUSE THEY DID NOT POSSESS THE LOVE OF TRUTH THAT COULD HAVE SAVED THEM ..."

This is not only THE most accurate description of the Modernists: this 'loss of love of Truth' also describes the Priests who, out of fear of the Modernist priests and bishops, have decided to go soft on the teachings of the Holy Church, and to comply with the fundamental request of the WCC: 'to stick only to that which is common to all the other denominations'. This, as all those 'who kept a great love of Truth', and so can tell you all about RENEW and the RITE OF CHRISTIAN INITIATION (RCIA), is precisely zilch, ZERO!

But pinpointing would not be what it is, if it was not precise. In addition to placing the closing stages of the times of the Gentiles in the broader (but very telling) context of a universal corruption and a great loss of Love, God in His infinite mercy has accommodated the the human craving for 'signs and wonders'. Using kind of a divine zooming-lens, He has placed 'the end' in the close-up of the narrow context of a much greater precision. By focusing our attention on Jerusalem, He placed 'the end of the Gentiles' in the context of dates and times and seasons, when His Son declared 'that Jerusalem will be trampled underfoot until the times of the Gentiles are completely over'.

When was Jerusalem 'delivered from pagan rule'? When was the material fulfilment of the prophecy, i.e. the obvious end of the treading down? It gets less than a one-line mention on p.240 of Prof. Carroll Quigley's monumental book, "Tragedy and Hope", 'A History of the World in our Time', out of a total of some 1350 pages! The one line reference reads:

> "Jerusalem fell to General Allenby in December 1917."

It meant the end of Moslem dominance since 636 A.D., when Abu Obieda had laid siege to Jerusalem and took it from the Romans. Not long after Obeida's victory OMAR arrived on the scene to complete the transfer and to give instructions for the building of the mosque on the side of the Temple, bearing his name: the beginning of the 'treading down' of Jerusalem by the pagans.

And now that we know the first part of the fulfilment of our Lord's prophecy: the year-of-the-end of the treading down of Jerusalem, the second part of His prediction: "the end of the times of the Gentiles" has now been pinpointed: the year of FATIMA. According to Our Blessed Lord, the deliverance of Jerusalem from pagan dominance ends 'the times of the Gentiles'.

What is it then, that the Catholic Nations of the world, the Gentiles, have done since 1917 which makes it just as obvious that their times have come to an end as it is obvious that Jerusalem has been delivered from pagan rule? What have they done? Since the great Apparitions of Our Lady at FATIMA, the Western Nations have rejected Her call to repentance. And with the rejection of Fatima, that is, with the calculated "banishment of the Woman into the desert of oblivion" (Rev. 12:6, 14), the West has finally sealed its doom: the times of the Gentiles have definitely come to an end: their role had been fulfilled.

In the plan of God FATIMA was the final call for the Christian Nations of the world to victimhood. To remember their Catholic beginning and their vocation to 'stand in' for the conversion of others, as the Holy Mother of God had once done for them at the foot of the Cross. But the West was to engrossed in its materialism to heed the call. As Teilhard observed in the 1929 description of his own defection in 'The Human Sense': "No one has been able to rekindle a love that has burned out ..."

So, when the signal for the end of the times of the Gentiles has been clearly given in 1917, then 'camping outside the Catholic Church' in 1991 on a non-existing strip of 'peaceful coexistence' in abject fear of the Modernists, must be classed as an act akin to 'spiritual suicide'! No wonder Our Lord called the virgins 'foolish', who, as the proto-type of all such foolish people, were forced to watch in mounting horror and desperation their own exclusion when, they were not where they should have been at a very late hour ...

Like Our Lord, St. Paul too predicts 'the end of the Gentiles' and again, like Our Lord, puts it squarely in relation to 'the Jewish phenomenon' without mentioning Jerusalem. But with that he has for anyone who lives in the second half of the twentieth century pinpointed with equal clarity when the 'times of the Gentiles' have come to a close. For 'the Jewish question' is still the dominant question in the Middle East and would not have remained the most elusive one for the West to solve had the Western nations not lost their original love for the Catholic Church, having now become 'as blind as the Jews are', and for exactly the same reason.

> "One section of Israel has become blind, but this will only last until the Gentiles have entered, and then after this the remnant of Israel will be saved as well." (Rom. 11:25-26)

Of the second, will the universal lawlessness be accompanied by an EXODUS from the Catholic Church?

It is not hard to imagine that the disillusionment of the European Gentiles with their Holy Mother the Catholic Church would result in Her abandonment, i.e. that the original influx would turn into an outflow. However, the fact that the growing number of Western Catholics who since 1968 have turned their backs on the Church by adopting contraceptive and homosexual lifestyles, and who with many of their priests have been clamouring ever since for reforms incompatible with their Catholic identity, without physically leaving the Church, would have given the wrong impression but for the timely arrival of a man of God who was at once both a Pope and a Saint.

Pope St. Pius X died in 1914, three years before FATIMA, which can truly be seen as a corroboration of his lifelong work "to restore everything in Christ". It was given to this great Pontiff to identify the impending universal lawlessness and loss of love for the Church of Western Catholics already rooted in Modernism, as an exodus from Her, when in a Letter to the whole Church, i.e. with Christ's authority, he called what he saw by its proper name: 'the great movement of apostasy organised in every country'. The full impact of this will only be felt if it is realised that only Catholics can apostatise and that 'this great movement of apostasy' has thus been identified by him as a movement inside the Church but for a wholesale exodus from Her. And with this, a tangible separation has thus become immaterial! And because Christ could depend on His future good friend to do his duty, no more needed to be said by Him. If Christ could give His authority in our times to see the universal lawlessness and loss of love identified as an apostasy, i.e. an exodus from the Church He founded, it must have been already part of the description He gave when, gazing at the temple of Jerusalem, He talked with His friends about the things He saw before His eyes, things that were to take place before His return at the end of time.

Of the third, where will this outflow end up? Can the receptacle to receive it be as easily identified as the exodus itself?

When Pope St. Pius X identified for us the universal lawlessness and loss of love for the Catholic Church by many of Her children as 'the great movement of apostasy, organised in every country', he did not stop there, but went on immediately to identify for us the receptacle that was being envisaged to receive this 'catholic' outflow. As we already know, this is what he wrote:

"This organisation which formerly afforded such promising expectations, has been harnessed in its course by the modern enemies of the Church, and is now no more than a miserable effluent of the great movement of apostasy, being organised in every country for the establishment of a One-World Church, which shall have neither dogmas nor hierarchy neither discipline of the mind nor curb for the passions, and which, under the pretext of freedom and human dignity, would bring back to the world the reign of legalised cunning and brute force and of the oppression of the weak and of all those who toil and suffer".

"We know only too well the dark workshops in which are elaborated these mischievous doctrines which ought not seduce clear thinking minds."[5]

---

[5] Pope St. Pius X. *Our Apostolic Mandate.* 1910.

From the characteristics the author of this Letter is at pains to spell out for us, we clearly see it to be his intention to impress on us that this world-wide organisation is an Anti-Church, the church of Antichrist. But Antichrist, known as 'the first beast of the Apocalypse', uses his 'church', (the second beast), for its own political purposes and for the destruction of all Revealed Religion. Since the World Council of Churches (which in spite of its name is universally known to be a very political animal) is the only world-wide organisation in existence today capable, ready and only too eager to absorb this big, catholic outflow, that is, to accommodate apostates, it is very tragic but inevitable, that the World Council of Churches is now identified with this One-World Church of Pope St. Pius X. And so, as the 'church of the great movement of apostasy', has become revealed to us as being 'the Church of Antichrist', 'the second beast of the Apocalypse'. For that reason, not only the name: the One-World Church, and not only all the hallmarks given here by Pope St. Pius X to this 'church', but even the name and the characteristics attached by St. John to 'the second beast' must now by necessity be transferred to the World Council of Churches, called into existence for the destruction of all Revealed Truth.

According to someone in the know,[6] "the stakes are high, very high ..."

> "The goal of the boldest ecumenical thinkers and leaders has grown increasingly clear: to construct a world community embracing all races, classes, religions and political systems, and to unite them as far as possible under a common world government whose business it will be to establish of world peace. It is hoped that a universal church will be able to pave the way successfully for a one-world government. Such a universal church would, however, not only be trans-confessional, it would also be unconditionally open to partnership with other religions and ideologies. If anyone stands in the way of this new religious-political view of Missions today; he is wooed in a friendly manner, simply passed

---

[6] Prof. Peter Beyerhaus in his incredible book "Bangkok '73'.

over as unimportant, or, if these methods are not effective, wrathfully attacked."

If that was as clear as this in 1973, it has become irreversible in 1991. Who is Professor Peter Beyerhaus?

In 1974 there appeared on the world scene an English translation of an incredible German book, written by a Lutheran Doctor in Theology in 1973, which book dispelled any doubts many of us may still have had about the religious future of the world. The title of the book is "Bangkok '73", and its author Prof. Dr. Peter Beyerhaus. If anyone still needs convincing that Modernism is conceived in hell, this book will achieve that.

Dr. Peter Beyerhaus is one of that rare breed of international theologians still wholly uncontaminated by modernism, and his book "Bangkok '73" is an eyewitness account of what actually took place before AND at the Eighth Conference on World Mission, held at Bangkok in 1973, under the auspices of the World Council of Churches. The title for this World Conference on Missions was, significantly enough, SALVATION TODAY.

In his book, Prof. Beyerhaus explains to us the unbelievable but TOTAL contradiction that took place at the Conference: how 326 serious, mission-minded delegates can come together to study the ADVANCE of global missionary activity, and can come out with the exact opposite: calling for a HALT, a MORATORUIM on missionary activity, thinking honestly they were still the same people, and that they were doing God and the missions are good turn.

In these few lines lies the most accurate description one could ever hope to give of RENEW, expressing in its brevity the most fundamental objection the Holy Church could ever have against it.

Prof. Beyerhaus meets the question head-on. "The true key" he says "to the planning of the course, and to the full understanding of the Bangkok Conference itself lies in the professed 'equation' between a systematically staged socio-psychological experiment (group dynamics: 'brainwashing') and the action of the Holy Spirit".

And the professor then sets out to show from every angle and with a welter of detail how this perversion 'of equating brainwashing with the Holy

Spirit' was carried out. Nothing was left to chance! Even the objection that such an exercise is impossible is squarely met. The poor delegates did not have a chance from the word go. Why? BECAUSE THEY BECAME INVOLVED.

And judging by the innumerable Catholics who now believe the opposite of what the Church taught us before, who no longer can tell the difference between Catholic Faith and any other faith, and who think that 'being on the pill' and accepting *Humanae Vitae* can go together: the experiment did not stop at Bangkok, but has swept the world.

In describing all the aspects of how the basic rules of brainwashing were applied at Bangkok, Prof. Beyerhaus lays bare THE most crucial, central brandmark of RENEW, stamped on it by its psychologist 'father' Robert Newsome: "the complete mutual openness, so that people can expose their vulnerability without questioning". He quotes Dr. Hoffman in an interview for the South West German Radio:

> "We hope that there are enough people here who are vulnerable, and who will let them-

selves be wounded, so that they can hear the strange things and the unheard of things <u>which have never yet been heard</u> that others will say to them ..."

And Prof. Beyerhaus' comment:

"This meant that we should be ready to call all the convictions in question, and all the presuppositions we brought with us, and even that we should abandon them in order to open ourselves up to the 'unheard of things', perhaps even that <u>which contradicts our Christian Faith</u>."

When the white delegates "became involved" and accepted this condition, and were subsequently confronted by the coloured delegates with all the evils of 'colonialism' and with the 'evils of missionary activities carried out in name of colonialism', the stony-faced white delegates were eventually <u>made to feel</u> so crushed that they not only became ashamed of their colour, but ever so much more importantly for the marxists staging the show (and for Satan behind them) became ashamed of their Christian religion. And to make up for the evils done, they voted for the moratorium on mission activity.

And that is how Catholic 'involvement' with RENEW opens the mind to the WCC, and to pitching camp outside the Church ...

Summary of Chapter Four

Chapter Four is the most critical one in this little book. If the first three chapters deal with the Catholic view of a world organisation wholly outside the Catholic Church, Chapter Four deals with the strong and inevitable links Catholics have with this organisation, if, out of fear of Modernism, they do not oppose it. For, according to the stern and numerous warnings of Pope St. Pius X against Modernism, the Modernists are no longer part of the Catholic Church even if, like leeches, they still have attached themselves to the Mystical Body of Christ. And since the WCC is the only worldwide vessel in existence eager and capable to receive them, they are part of the WCC. Modernists make ideal members!

If not opposing Modernism, 'many' Catholics (the word is used by Christ) show that they have lost much of their love for their Holy Mother the Catholic Church. They pretend that they live in a kind of 'no-man's land' of 'peaceful coexistence' between the two warring forces of the 'everlasting enmity'. But for a number of reasons, this 'peaceful coexistence' does not exist, and so neither does this 'no-man's land'! In not wishing to be part of God's side of the warring forces, they are condemned to be part of the other. And the other side is diabolical enough to equate brainwashing and group dynamics with 'the action of the Holy Spirit'.

This is borne out with alarming speed in everyday life. Even good priests who have allowed themselves to be cast in this mould, always bow before and towards the strong demands of Modernism. They never seem to take a strong stand on the demands of the Church. They speak of salvation in such a way that people easily get the impression that it is inevitable. Christ is always portrayed as having taken care of everything. What is required of Catholics in response is not even minimally spelled out.

And so people are peacefully left in their sins ... This is the worst state to find oneself in 'if indeed the times of the Gentiles have come to a close'. Those who could have entered the Holy Catholic Church and did not leave Her, are IN. Those who left Her, either permanently as Modernist apostates (Pope St. Pius X), or have 'temporarily' taken up camp outside Her on that fatal strip of 'no-man's land' so as not to be too closely identified with Her out of fear for the Modernists, are (or could find themselves) locked OUT!

Chapter Five

The Church of the New Age

The foregoing has spelled out the terrible end awaiting all Catholics who truly think that the church has changed and has changed sufficiently for them to take matters into their own hands, to fill the vacancy left by Her 'uncertainty' and to do as they please. Still, the shadow of their doom is not yet the end of the story.

There is plenty of evidence around for anyone to be horrified by the true nature of Modernism, yet few Catholics show any sign that they <u>are</u> horrified. The majority of Catholics including many good Priests refuse to give it the "Everlasting Enmity" it deserves. Adhering to the bottom-line of their lives: "What's the use!", they accommodate it, and in refusing to fight it and to resist it with all their might, they shun the people who do. By making apologies for their lack of resistance, they are forced to rationalise their position and to make allowances for Modernism. And they fail to see that now they are in a 'protection racket', that they have lost the freedom of the children of God, and that they are paying big money to extortionists in return for being 'left alone'. They are willing to pay their priests with 'popularity', and the priests are prepared to accept it, as long as both camps understand each other and leave each other peacefully "in their sin". The bottom line of their lives is not Faith, or Love, but FEAR! And the clear end result – as in all such cases – is, that they will NOT be left alone ....

This is the sort of stuff that produces 'peaceful coexistence', displaced persons camped in between two warring forces, waiting for hand-outs from either side. It is never the stuff that produces fierce freedom fighters, victimhood, reparation and leadership. And at its worst, this 'peaceful coexistence' racket is the breeding ground from which the enemy recruits its 'Quislings', those prepared to do the dirty work for them.

Yes, going by the unprecedented scale on which Modernism has engulfed the Church, the 'great movement of apostasy' was no misnomer in 1910, and 'the end of the time of the Gentiles' has not only been truly signalled but has come to pass ...

Chapter Five: The Church of the New Age

If 1917 was the year appointed by God "for the deliverance of Jerusalem", then by an unbreakable Divine Connection, it also contains the mystery surrounding the signal of "the end of the times of the Gentiles". It is not hard to see that this 'warning of the end' is intimately connected with the secret of the Six Apparitions of Our Blessed Lady at FATIMA. And that the secret of FATIMA must then essentially be seen as the final warning to the Gentiles "to remain in the Church and <u>how</u> to remain in the Church".

Fatima confirms all the Dogmas, the doctrines, and devotions which for 2000 years have set the Catholic Church apart from an other 'church' as the spiritual Mother of all mankind. In a mere Six Apparitions there were held up and stressed –

- The Blessed Trinity.
- The Divinity of Christ.
- The Real, bodily presence of Christ in the Blessed Eucharist.
- Mary Immaculate and Assumed into Heaven.
- The structured Church:

- Papacy,
- Bishops,
- Priests, and
- Laity.

- The existence of:

  - Life after death.
  - Heaven, Hell and Purgatory,
  - Grace and Sin.
  - Angels and devils.
  - A truly Catholic Tradition.

- The necessity of:

  - Penance and Reparation.
  - The Confession of Sins.
  - Frequent Communion.
  - The Daily Rosary.
  - The wearing of the Scapular.
  - Prayer.
  - Purity.

- The reality of Miracles.
- The meaning of suffering and victimhood.

- The Dogma of Divine Justice:

  o Reward for virtue
  o Punishment for sin.

For a catholic, this is the only way <u>how</u> to remain a Catholic; and for those outside the Church, this is the only way <u>how</u> to enter Her. If an RCIA programme does not contain this, it is a fraud! The Church which refuses to surrender any of the above in Her day-to-day teaching, and will not 'stick only to that which is common amongst the rest of the christian denominations' is the true Catholic Church founded by Christ. But the 'church' which does surrender the above out of fear of being expelled as a 'maverick church' by the rest of the christian denominations, can only be some Modernist counterfeit of the true Catholic Church.

Several important points can be raised here. E.g.

1. When was it that you, the reader, heard a good sermon on any of the above, let alone a systematic development? Twenty, thirty years ago? When old Dean so-and-so was still the Parish

Priest? Truly blessed are those who can say: 'We still have Parish Priests who deal with these on nearly every occasion'.

2. If one must confess 'Yes, it was some twenty, or thirty years ago since anyone of us heard a good sermon in our part of the Church on any of the things Our Lady brought to the world at FATIMA', then there are 'Two Fears', both unholy, which lie at the root of the eclipse.

One, the fear of losing touch with the 'people'(?), of losing popularity with the congregation and so driving them away to 'easy priests' who only waffle about 'luv' while leaving people safely in their sins, with a subsequent loss of revenue; the nagging fear of being laughed at, of being considered old-fashioned, of no longer 'making sense'; the real fear of being denounced to the Modernists and subsequently railroaded, resides mainly (but not exclusively) in priests and catholic 'intellectuals' (teachers!).

The other, the fear of losing one's newly-acquired freedom of decision making, of being 'forced' to follow again an 'informed' conscience, of being disturbed out of one's contraceptive lifestyle, resides mainly (but by no means exclusively) in the laity.

Both fears point to a loss of Catholic Faith, a loss of love, a loss of Catholic identity and so reveal a loss of cohesion with the Catholic Church in a very advanced stage: all signs of 'the end of the times of the Gentiles'.

3. By far the great majority of modern 'Catholics' who reject FATIMA will do so for the sole reason 'that it is merely a private revelation'. But coming in the year that signalled 'the end of the treading down underfoot of Jerusalem by the Gentiles', it was irrevocably bracketed within the Divine Prophecy 'as a warning for the nations of the pending end of the times of the Gentiles'. And Divine Ingenuity made it so, that the message of FATIMA could not be rejected without rejecting at the same time a 2000 year Tradition of the Holy Catholic Church. Our Lady, as 'the Woman of Genesis', is at the centre of 'The Everlasting Enmity'. Thus Our Blessed Lady cannot be rejected without turning one's back on the only side of 'The Everlasting Enmity' to which

the victory has been secured. And the war of 'The Everlasting Enmity' is fought here on earth by only ONE camp on the side of Our Lady: by the Church Militant.

Thus the active or passive rejection of FATIMA amounts to only One thing: to become an inextricably tangled-up Catholic in the web of the World Council of Churches.

The future is therefore bright. For the future belongs only to ONE Church: the ONE created in the spotless image and likeness of Her, who at FATIMA could so confidently predict:

"In the end My Immaculate Heart will triumph."

There will be only one 'New Age': the AGE OF MARY. And in that Golden Age there will be only one Church, the very Church who at this moment is fighting on Mary's side of "The Everlasting Enmity".

Summary of Chapter Five

FATIMA was the Divine Warning for the Gentile nations of the West "to remain in the Church and HOW to remain in the One, Holy, Catholic and Apostolic Church". For it signalled 'the end of the

Chapter Five: The Church of the New Age   97

times of the Gentiles', which would come to pass if the clear warning of true repentance was not heeded.

FATIMA cannot be set aside simply because it is merely a private revelation. If it is ignored for that reason, then its message must still be shouted from the rooftops, because FATIMA is a most wonderful recapitulation of 2000 years of Catholic teaching in the unique Catholic Tradition. FATIMA is an integral part of the fulfillment of Christ's prophecy in the Gospel of St. Luke 'about the end of the treading down of Jerusalem'. Since by this it has become part of the context in which Christ foretold 'the end of the times of the Gentiles', Our Lord has thus arranged matters in such a wonderful way, that FATIMA has truly become <u>Christ's</u> message to the Gentile nations of the West of 'how to remain in His Church', or face the consequences! With it, He has literally cleared the 'no-man's land' from all squatters.

But Fatima has done more. In ONE sentence, Our Lady has also gone directly to the heart of the modern problem, and given it its unique Catholic solution. When Our Lady said, "MANY souls go to

Hell because there is no one to pray or to bring sacrifices for them," she did three (3) things

1. She ripped the mask off the modern nonsense 'that salvation is guaranteed', that 'salvation is inevitable', and revealed to us underneath the mask the ugly face of Satan.
2. She revealed that MANY (the same word used by Our Lord in the same context of the universal apostasy) souls actually fall into Hell, not so much for what they have done, but because 'there is no one found to pray or to bring sacrifices for them'. In other words, not only <u>could</u> they have been saved, but they <u>should</u> have been saved! They are obviously not saved by the 'inevitability of salvation', but by 'victimhood': an heroic effort!
3. She addressed Herself to all those Catholics camped 'a certain distance away' from the Catholic Church awaiting 'safer times', telling them that, while they were saving their own skin, others, who had been entrusted to their prayers and sacrifices, were falling into Hell: the strongest motive for all those Catholics to break up camp

and to return to the practise of a virile, lively, Faith!

Yes, indeed, that 'no-man's land' should have been cleared of all squatters, but is it? And will they have time to return?

Epilogue

In two places in his latest, most explicit and comprehensive encyclical "The Mission of the Redeemer", in the Section called "Mission 'Ad Gentes'", our present Holy Father Pope John Paul II refers specifically to the defection of the Christian Nations, mentioning Europe in particular. And it is here that the Pope makes the fundamental distinction between 'Gentes' and 'Gentiles'. The later, 'the Gentiles' are the pagans of Apostolic times to whom the Apostle of the Gentiles addressed himself, on his own admission, "to make my own people, the Jews, jealous". (Rom. 11:14). It is these 'Gentiles' who flocked into the Church and thus became the foundation of Catholic Europe, and of the christianisation of 'the West' in general. And it is of these 'Gentiles' that Christ predicted "that their times would come to an end"; of whom Pope St. Pius X warned "that they would become part of a great movement of apostasy in every country for the establishment of a 'One-World Church'", and of whom the present Holy Father now writes:

"Nor are difficulties lacking within the People of God: Indeed, these difficulties are the most painful of all. As the first of these difficulties Pope Paul VI pointed to 'the lack of fervour which is all the more serious because it comes from within. It is manifested in fatigue, disenchantment, compromise, lack of interest, and above all lack of joy and hope'. Other great obstacles (as if the foregoing were not enough!) to the Church's missionary work include past and present divisions among Christians, de-christianisation within Christian countries ... the counter witness of believers ..." [36]. And, "Today, the majority of believers are no longer found in Europe ... The ends of the earth to which the Gospel must be brought are growing ever more distant." [40]

These are the 'Gentes', the pagan peoples, to whom the 'Gentiles', must bring the Kingdom of God, but to whom instead is so often being proclaimed 'the One-World Church' because of the 'counter-witness of the Christian nations'. It is be-

Epilogue

cause of all these difficulties, that the Holy Father must state that "the ends of the earth to which the Gospel must be brought ARE GROWING EVER MORE DISTANT", while according to his own observation, the world is getting smaller ...

So, while the 'Gentiles': Europe and the Christan nations, will suffer for their defection because of what he Holy Father calls 'their counter-witness', the 'Gentes' will benefit from the springtime of the new Pentecost: the glory of having the Kingdom of God proclaimed to them unpolluted, in spite of the 'counter-witness' of the latest 'church' of the 'Gentiles': the 'One-World Church' of the World Council of Churches.

www.ingramcontent.com/pod-product-compliance
Lightning Source LLC
Chambersburg PA
CBHW070854050426
42453CB00012B/2192